101 Healing Blessings

Words of Comfort and Strength
for Your Journey to Wellness

Lauren Lulu Taylor
Forward & Illustrations by Daisy Taylor

UP

UPLIFTERS PRESS

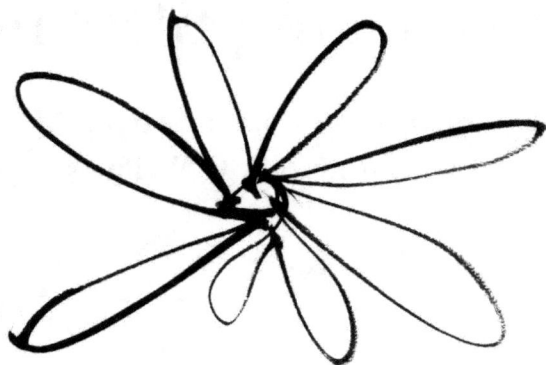

For Daisy

FORWARD

The nurse came to my bedside in the crowded recovery room. I did not know what was wrong with me. Neither did she. She took both my hands in hers and looked me square in the eye. "Give yourself," she said, "a little grace."

Some time or other. Sooner or later. We all need a little grace.

It does not have to be part of a belief system, or even come from someone you know. But it could be a kiss from your dog, or any dog for that matter, or a heart drawn on your coffee cup by the barista. A paper-folded origami crane, found near the bus stop.

A blessing in any form, by any name at all, will surround you with kindness. For a moment. And soften the world just a little.

Sometimes you need a blessing just to take the next step or to speak the next word. We all have those times and those moments.

When I was in treatment, my sister emailed me a blessing every morning from the other side of the world. And even when she came to visit me, she still wrote me a blessing every day. And when she had to go home again, she still wrote me a blessing every day.

Every day, I got myself up knowing that I would find a blessing waiting for me. I read them aloud to myself before I did anything else... even on the days when I couldn't do much of anything else.

It was a remarkable gift she gave to me, but I hoped that one day those blessings could reach others too. When she suggested she might put them in a book, I was overjoyed.

And here it is...

Daisy Taylor
Cancer-free

INTRODUCTION

Welcome to "101 Healing Blessings: Words of comfort and strength for your journey to wellness."

This book is a simple offering created to accompany you on your path to well-being. Rooted in the universal belief that words and positive affirmations hold transformative powers, especially when spoken, this non-denominational anthology aspires to offer you solace and strength.

"101 Healing Blessings" serves as an acknowledgment of the profound impact words can wield on our healing journey — a recognition that blessings weave through the fabric of diverse cultures and religions. Whether you find sanctuary in traditional faith or draw strength from the universal currents of spirituality, these blessings intentionally resist confinement to any particular denomination. They are presented here as a gift for all — a gesture of hope and encouragement as you navigate the intricacies of your health challenges.

As you turn these pages, allow your voice to breathe life into these blessings. May the words you need most find you when you need them.

"A blessing is a circle of light drawn around a person to protect, heal and strengthen."

— John O'Donohue

You are alive.

With every inhale,
With every exhale,
You stand as a living testament.

Strong heart,
You are a survivor.

May you find kindness within, especially in moments of suffering.

May the words you speak to yourself be filled with love and patience.

May you be your own lover and your most loyal friend.

May you grant yourself compassion and the understanding you deserve.

And, above all, may you delight in the music of your own laughter.

3

May you find a quiet haven in the gentle words
of this blessing,
a soft reminder that you are more than
your physical difficulties,
more than the challenges you face today.

Outside the contours of bed and couch,
in the recesses of your mind, spirit, and existence,
may you stretch beyond this singular moment.

Allow this blessing to permeate your being,
resonating with the truth
that you are more.

You're blessed, worthy, and infinitely loved.

May comfort find you in the understanding
that your essence surpasses the challenges you face.
You are not confined by this struggle,
but shaped by the spirit that persists within you.

You're blessed, worthy, and infinitely loved.

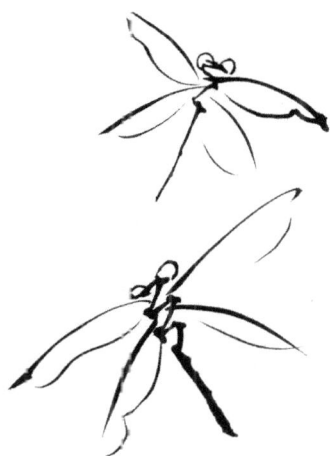

4

Go lightly, go lightly—be gentle with yourself.

In this moment, there is nothing you need to do.

No judgment, just be.

Let go of worries—the need to 'do'.

Some days, it is simply enough to look out the window,

to bow your head in respect to the face in the mirror,

to lay your head down on the pillow—knowing

healing is working its way quietly all around you.

In quiet moments, there is unseen progress,

Standing still, blind to distance, out of sight.

May tranquil pauses be your guiding light,

As change quietly gathers strength in the still of night.

In the hibernation of the moment, change is sown,

Roots of renewal.

Silently, like the tide,

Change gathers force.

Within the stillness, a marathon is run,

Step by step, the journey is won.

Impossible dreams, make them plausible,
In the space of healing, find the possible.

In the face of challenges, stand hopeful and true,
Impossible is possible when belief is in you.

Strength does not reside in muscle or limb,
It emanates from the will, a light within.

Despite each stumble, still a chance to soar,
Take heart, your path has much left to explore.

Fall nine times, stand up once more.
In the cadence of comeback, spirit will restore.

May you be patient, let time unfold its art,
For joy comes after sorrow, mending every broken part.

May you be blessed beyond measure,
In the messy, imperfect moments.

May grace find you when you're lost in the chaos of life,
And guide you through the darkest struggles.

May you let go of expectations and perfection's demand,
Surrender to life, unfolding, unplanned.

May you embrace your flaws, your scars, your quirks,
For in our imperfections, true beauty dwells.

And may you always know, in the depths of your soul,
That you are loved, cherished, and allowed to grow.

Stars above so bright,
Bring peace in the quiet night,
Healing with their light.

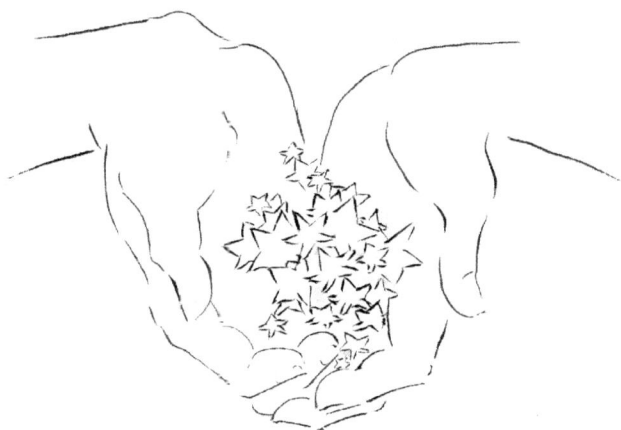

May you find solace in the simple joys that surround,
A cup of warm tea to wrap your hand around.

May you savor each moment, both big and small,
Finding gratitude, even when life seems to stall.

When you stumble, and fall, as we often do,
May you find the strength to rise anew.

For in vulnerability and rising after defeat,
We find resilience, growth, and stories to repeat.

May you find peace in knowing you are never alone,
Surrounded by love, wherever you may roam.

Dearest one, may you embrace this blessed day,
With all its uncertainties and challenges,
Know that you are seen, valued, and truly loved,
A kindred spirit, forever connected, forever restored.

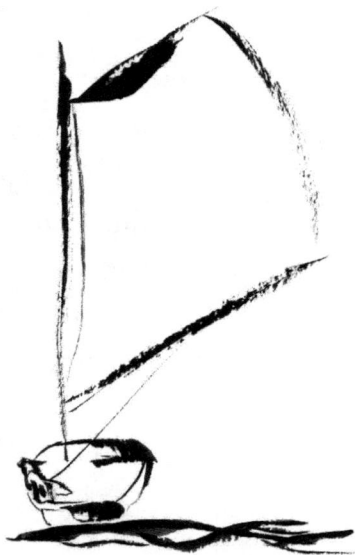

In the warmth of the nest where ship and sky meet in silent communion, may you find the courage to navigate the unknown seas of futurity.

May the warmth in the hold of your heart be a beacon, navigating uncharted seas, may you reach for a soft landing, a place where aspirations meet reality.

As you traverse the vast expanse between body and spirit, may you be led through toils and struggles.

In this sacred journey, may you transcend mere existence, may you discover the beauty of your own vessel.

May every cell radiate with healing light,
Restoring balance, strength, and renewed might.

May your bones be strong, your muscles enduring,
Your heart in rhythm, reassuring.

May your breath be deep, your lungs be clear,
A reminder that you are present, here.

May your heart beat steady, with love as its song,
Nourishing your body, steadfast and strong.

May your mind be calm, free from stress and strife,
Embracing clarity, giving steadiness in life.

May each step you take be filled with grace,
Moving with purpose, at your own pace.

May your spirit take wing, in harmony with your being,
Unveiling inner wisdom, foreseeing.

And as you walk the path of health and well-being,
May you find joy, fulfillment, and true meaning.

On this day, when the world is touched by light,
And breath flows through you,
Pause and recognize the simple miracle
Of being alive.

Regardless of the challenges that cross your path,
Let every inhale, every heartbeat declare: You are
Alive.

May you be blessed with radiant health.
May your body be strong.
May your mind be clear and your spirit uplifted.

May you experience well-being in every aspect of your life.
May you be free from illness and disease.
May your immune system be robust and resilient.

May you find joy and contentment in taking care of yourself.
May you be blessed with a long, happy, and healthy life.

In the contemplation of the question, "why me?" you find yourself standing at the threshold of uncertainty.

Answers may remain elusive.

The road you tread may twist and turn, at times veering sharply into the unknown.

May each unforeseen challenge become a testament
to your endurance,
a marker of your indomitable spirit.

Moon soft and bright,
Healing in its tranquil light,
Restoring hopeful dreams.

When shadows of illness cast their spell,
In silent moments when tears fall,
May you know that you are not alone.

When you feel lost and out of place,
When it seems you can't carry on,
May you know you are not alone.

Amidst the whirlwind, disruptive forces,
The chaos unfolding, the uncertainties shown,
May you know you are not alone.

As you read these lines, let the truth be known,
Deep in your bones, inside your heart,
You will never be alone as long as you are loved,
And you, dear one, are so deeply loved.

May you receive each moment as a gift,
Understanding that even darkness has its purpose.

May challenges be invitations to grow,
Vulnerability, a path worth bravely revealing.

May you drink in beauty in every space.

Shine in the world with your gentle light.

May you be protected.

May you prosper amid the ebb and flow.

Blessings to you, dear one, in every hour.

May you find joy in the simplest of things,
In laughter, in love.

May your creativity flow, wild and free,
Breathing life into art.

And when darkness casts its shadow,
May you always find the strength,
To persevere,
The light to leave fear behind.

Blessings upon you, brave heart,
As you walk this earthly land,
May you find serenity.

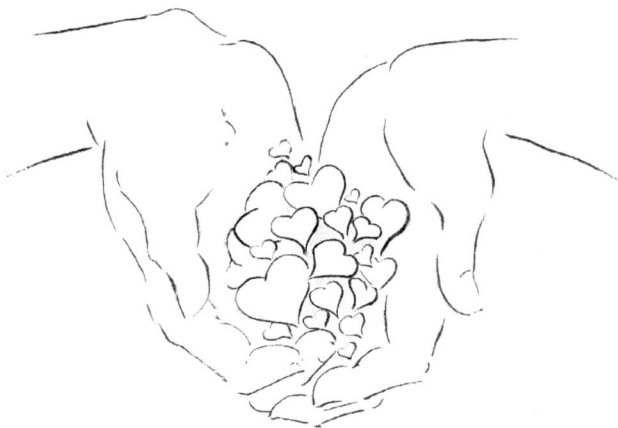

May your inner voice resonate: you are more than enough.

May your steps be light, as you walk the earth,
Reveling in the miracle of each moment's worth.

May the sun's gentle rays kiss your skin,
Reviving your spirit, from deep within.

May the winds reveal secrets of vitality and life,
Guiding you through any struggle or strife.

May this blessing wrap all around you,
With love and care to see you through.

May the world bless you with its wildness,
The untamed beauty that makes your heart sing.

May you walk through meadows and forests,
Feel the pulse of nature, in every living thing.

May you swirl with the wind, swift and free,
Let it carry your dreams to distant shores.

May you drink from rivers of endless inspiration,
And explore your thirst for more, even more.

May your toes touch the wavelets, shell to your ear,
As oceans unveil secrets and tales untold.

May you find solace in their vastness, their flow,
And discover the depths of your untamed soul.

May the Earth bless your footsteps,
May you find your own pace.

In this intricate web of life,
May you find your own place.

26

May your day be uneventful.

In the quiet sanctuary of your inner being,
May you find solace, in the midst of healing.

May each breath you take be a soothing balm,
Easing your burdens, bringing peace and calm.

May your body mend with graceful ease,
As strength and vitality steadily increase.

May your spirit rise, resilient and strong,
Unfolding like a bird's graceful song.

In the depths of night, may stars guide your way,
Illuminating the path to a brighter day.

Within you, a wellspring of strength does reside,
Know you can draw on that inner might.

Let the sun's warm rays guide your way,
Illuminating a path to a brighter day.

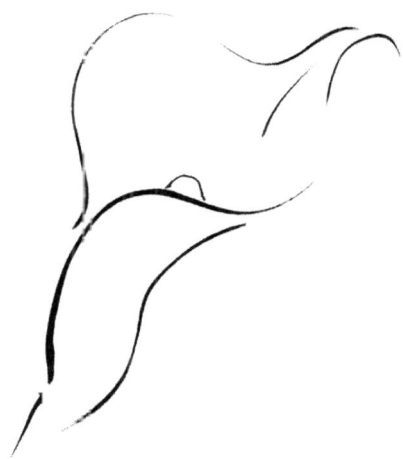

May your body be a sanctuary of healing.
May every breath infuse you with strength.
May the gentle touch of kindness mend you.

May your spirit find solace and your heart peace.
May every step you take be filled with perseverance.
May the light within you shine brighter each day.

With each heartbeat, may you find strength anew.
May the blessings of health always be with you.
May the song of resilience be the anthem of your days.

In healing's gentle sway,
Where light and shadow spin and wind,
Find solace along the way,
Grace and wellness intertwined.

Your body, like a canvas, new,
With brushstrokes of healing each day,
A masterpiece of health shines through,
Guided by love in a gentle way.

In the intricate weave of life's design,
May healing threads weave firm and sure,
Mending the fabric of body and mind,
Restoring wholeness, an embrace pure.

You are a beautiful soul, may your life be blessed.

32

Some days may surge, like storms unfurl,
Others so gentle, a psalm, a pearl.

Today's a cosmic shrug, a unique healing dance,
What tomorrow brings may be a new twist of chance.

Amid chaos, let there be serene calm,
Some days a burden, others around the corner, a healing balm.

On this day, may you stand resilient,
In life's fluctuating currents, find healing brilliance.

In the ordinary, unearth the divine,
Where, centered, your heart will radiate and shine.

May you be surrounded by a community of love,
Supporting you from below and above.

May you embrace the dawn.

In the realm of silence, the body mends,
With each heartbeat.

With tranquil breath and steady grace,
Finding solace.

In the dance of stars and moon above,
Feel the power of boundless love,
Breathe it in, let it fill your soul,
As healing currents make you whole.

May you wake with the sun's first light,
And find yourself healthy.

May strength embrace you, day by day,
In body and mind.

May laughter ring in your heart,
Banishing aches and pains.

May you know in every breath you take,
You are loved in this world.

Let tender winds gently mend,
The wounds that time and troubles send.

With every step, a sacred dance,
A rhythm woven, like romance,
May each movement bring relief,
And soothe your soul, release your grief.

Through trials faced, a deeper glow,
A story of scars that show,
The courage in your spirit's flight,
A testament to your inner light.

In stillness discovered, a tranquil shore,
Where worries fade, and fears ignore,
Your boat propelled by a gentle breeze,
On a healing journey homeward, with ease.

May you be peaceful.
May you be free from harm.
May you be filled with loving kindness.

In every cell, a universe,
An orchestra of life, immersed,
May harmony restore your core,
And bring you health forevermore.

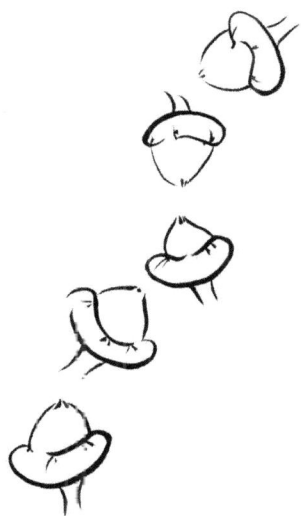

In the wisdom of silence, may answers arise,
And healing's enigma, within you, surprise.

A Birthday Blessing

With each new sunrise, may you awaken refreshed,
Embracing each day with positivity and zest.

May your heart be light, your mind be clear,
As you move through life's chapters, year after year.

May your birthday be a reminder of the strength you possess,
A celebration of health, happiness, and progress.

May you continue to shine with a radiant light,
Knowing in your heart that everything is alright.

In the gentle embrace of each new day,
May your body and spirit find their way.

May healing touch your soul,
As tender waves of wellness roll.

May each breath you take be a healing tide,
Guiding you to a place where worries subside.

With every step, may your health renew,
Vibrant as the sky of blue.

In the quiet spaces of your heart,
May a healing flower
bloom again.

Embrace the new day,
Golden rays of strength emerge,
Healing like sunrise.

May each breath you take be a healing psalm,
Infusing your being with tranquility and calm.

May your steps be light, as you walk the earth,
Reveling in the miracle of each moment's worth.

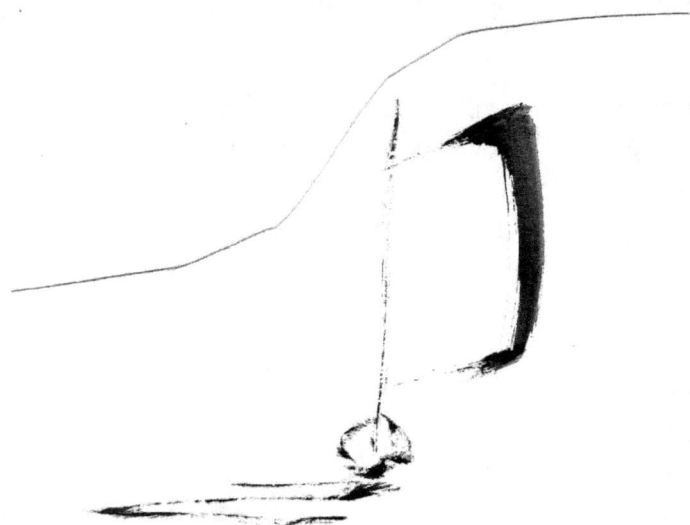

May no storm, darkness, or pain reach you,
May each breath bring renewal, healing on cue.

On the days when your shoulders feel leaden,
May no burden or sadness deaden.

May the wet and grey swiftly depart from you,
May a warm wind wrap you in words loving and true.

Renewal unfurls.
Gentle breeze of health.
Whispers through each breath you take.

In the dance of your own fragility,
May you recognize your strength,
For it is through brokenness
That we become whole.

In the quiet spaces of your soul,
May healing gently grow.
A tender touch to every part,
A soothing, steady flow.

May strength arise within you,
Like a river's steady roll,
Embracing every fiber,
Bringing vigor, soft and slow.

May you find solace in the gentle rituals of life – the tender
touch of water on your face, the peeling of a tangerine,
the comforting hug as you slip your feet into warm slippers.

Let the cool touch of your pillowcase against your cheek
be a reminder of the tangible normality that surrounds you.

May you root yourself in the here and now, finding peace
in simply being.

May healing hands,
Both near and far,
Guide you like a shining star.
In body, mind, and spirit, too,
May health and wholeness blossom in you.

Stand before the mirror, embrace your story bold and bright.
May you behold with love the beauty time cannot rewrite.

Inside lies true beauty, just out of view.
May you see resilience in every shade and hue.

May a deeper vision be your enduring cure,
As the mirror reveals your true face—radiant and pure.

There is no greater beauty than beauty's inner glow,
Luminescent and divine, from your heart it is bestowed.

Silent moon above,
Cradles dreams of hope and love,
Healing from the skies.

Beneath the stars,
Healing thoughts take flight and fly,
In dreams, we touch the sky.

May every sunrise, be a chance to renew,
To create a path that's uniquely you.

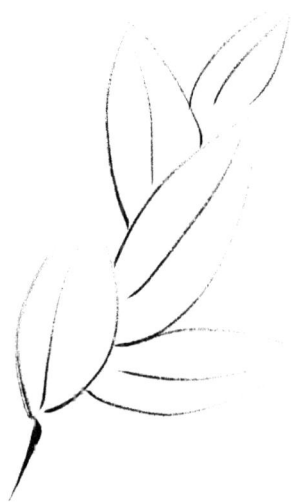

May healing find you in the quiet moments:

May your body mend,
Your spirit ascend,
Your soul transcend.

Within your mind's embrace,
All that you are takes place,
Your thoughts, like seeds in the soul's fertile ground,
Grow into deeds, silent and profound.

Positive echoes, vibrations, healing and bright,
Constructive musings, building valor and might.

May your thoughts mold your fate,
May you become an open slate.

Rustlings from the trees,
Give curative intentions,
Nature's remedies.

May you feel no shame in the tears you shed,
For they water the soil where resilience is bred.

May your tears be embraced, a cleansing rain,
Fostering kindness, washing away pain.

After tears fall, may transformation take flight,
Unveiling beauty, revealing insight.

It's painful to part with who you were before,
But in embracing then and now, you open.

May you entwine your former self with your present one,
Endure and expand, a journey not yet finished
has room for growth.

In acceptance, may you find the strength to hold on and let go,
A continuum of self, lessons, and blessings.

May you hold the contradiction of then and now,
Find the vastness in your own being.

In the echoes of shattered worlds, you've found your way,
Time and again, facing dawn after disarray.

The weight of brokenness, a burden you've borne,
Up from the floor, a spirit reborn.

A bit damaged, a bit cracked, yet whole
Your resilience, a story to extol.

Carry on, brave soul.

Stay true to your path, heart bold, spirit bright.
May your steps be purposeful, your burden be light.

Illusions in the shadows, call them by name!
Keep your gaze forward, and in light proclaim.

Darkness holds only the power that we choose to lend,
May your strength and resolve steadily ascend.

May you not rage against grief and great tears,
But bless the conflicts, the dream-shattering fears.

Touched by fervent desire, shaped by the storms of strife,
In these moments, dear one, you're truly embracing life.

From elation to sorrow, let your feelings preside,
No apologies, dear one, for your human side.

Let emotions weave, through tranquility and strife,
Every pulse, every sensation shouts you're truly—Alive.

In moments when solitude weighs heavy,
May you sense life's quiet companionship.

May the air around you offer comfort,
A reminder that solitude is a healing refuge.

May you find the subtle hum of your being in silence,
A reminder you are connected to the heartbeat of life.

May you draw strength from the subtle expressions of nature,
In every breeze, every leaf, and every sky, life resonates.

May the quiet company of the elements bring solace,
May you find peace in the gentle hold of existence.

In the thoughtful soul's retreat to solitude, find resilience,
A warrior's companion, a source of strength in stillness.

Alone, let your soul immerse itself in the embrace of solitude,
In these moments, may you find power to rejuvenate.

In the face of challenges, remember this truth:

Oaks grow strong in winds that oppose,
Diamonds are born under pressure that imposes.

From coal's compression to crystals' birth,
Pressure creates gems, rare and of worth.

From the forge of adversity, courage takes flight,
As wings of resilience spread, embracing the fight.

So when difficulties come, and hardships persist,
May you know, strife and extraordinary beauty coexist.

On Receiving:

In the gentle glow of others' kindness, may you unearth
a reservoir of strength that transcends mere acceptance.

May your heart be a sanctuary, a sacred abode, embracing
the care bestowed by those extending their hands in support.

May you recognize that in receiving, you are not merely
a recipient of a gift, but a conduit for reciprocal love.

May you boldly say 'yes' to gifts and help offered,
understanding that in receiving gracefully,
you offer the greater gift.

In the quiet of the dawn, where shadows softly embark,
May faith be the bird that sings, even in the dark.

When day is done, regardless of highs and lows,
May you gently tuck it away in the archives of time.

May you close your eyes,
And give in to the serenity of the night,
For with each slumber, a fresh chapter unfolds.

May you welcome assistance from others
without guilt or shame,
for when you replace 'I' with 'we,'
you rewrite illness into wellness.

(*blessing is inspired by a quote attributed to Malcolm X*)

May you find the strength to embrace,
and trust your own voice
amidst the myriad of stories and well-intentioned advice.

Your journey is woven with the threads
of your unique experiences,
and within the gentle echoes of your heart resides
a compass,
steadfast,
ready to guide you.

There are days when the weight of existence becomes
an anchor, tethering the spirit.

Unwanted feelings may tiptoe
into the corridors of your consciousness,
sometimes eluding name.

In this dimming, may your heart find solace.

May compassion, with its nonjudgmental presence,
be your partner.

And may you know, this too shall pass.

May you always speak to yourself with a gentle voice,
tender care, and boundless love.

May you sow these words aloud again and again,
through the core of your being, and the minutes
of each wondrous day of your life.

I am blessed.
I am grateful.
I am love.
I am peace.

In the hush of healing hours,
May kindness rise.

May every ache and worry depart,
Replaced by the heart's calm strum.

May patience soften your journey's climb,
For healing takes its own sweet time.

May your journey towards wellness be guided by grace.

May every cell in your body radiate with vitality and strength.

You are deserving of good health,
and may you experience it fully.

May beautiful moments take residence in your body.

May you find solace in nature's embrace,
As the trees sway to the rhythm of your heart.

May the sun's warm rays kiss your skin,
Infusing you with energy and healing from within.

May the stars escort your sorrows into the night,
May the dawn sky infuse you with unwavering courage.

May you be held in the gentle arms of compassion,
Surrounded by love and support that knows no bounds.

May the winds of change carry away your worries and fears.
May you discover the profound wisdom that lies within.

May your days be filled with moments of joy and gratitude,
As you witness the miracles of your body's resilience.

May you find peace in the stillness of the present moment,
May your spirit dance with the boundless joy of a wildflower.

May your days be painted with the colors of love.
May your spirit be as unbreakable as the dome of sky above.

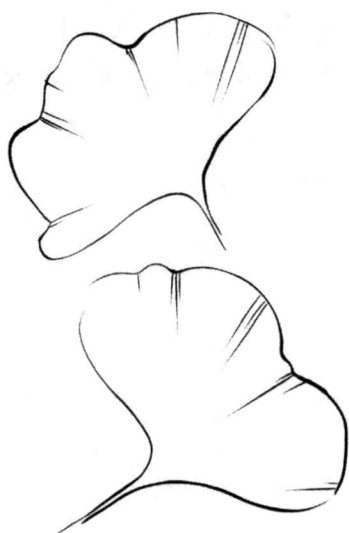

May sorrow be your guide sweeping away the clutter within.

May it gently remove the old, making space for the new.

May every moment of sadness transform into growth.

May the deepest pains hidden within you serve as
transformative medicine.

May change usher in a future better than you can imagine.

May what slips away from your life return renewed
and in a blessed form.

May your every breath build vitality,
Speaking words of healing and serenity.

May your heart beat with a rhythm of grace,
Nurturing love in every sacred space.

May your skin glow with the sun's tender kiss,
Receiving the warmth of life's gentle bliss.

May your days be a testament,
To the power of healing and fulfillment.

As the sun ascends, a new day unfurls,
Promising the subtle art of healing.

May each breath, be quiet renewal,
A chance for your body and soul to mend.

Moments pass, strength quietly returns,
Like a fragile bloom seeking the light.

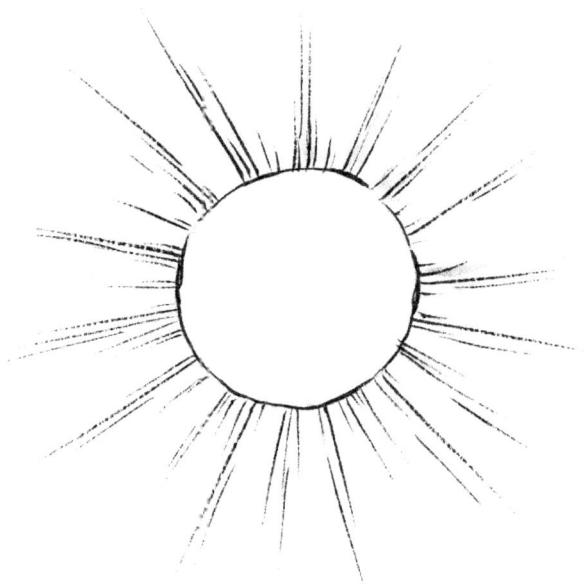

May the light of love illuminate your path,
May the gentle breeze of grace uplift your soul,
May the music of divine unity resonate within your heart,
May your journey be guided by the wisdom of the Universe.

Like the moon,
you are complete and enduring,
even when only a crescent sliver
of your brilliance
is visible to the world.

Breathing in, may you feel the essence of healing,
Every cell, every fiber, alive, revealing.

Breathing out, may you let go of all that's not well,
In this single moment, find your inner spell.

Within this tempest, may you find faith,
A silver lining, in the chaos.

May resilience rise, steadfast and strong,
A promise to rebuild.

May each affected life, its soul transform
Know
Tomorrow will be beautiful.

May each breath be a resonance of hope,
Each step forward, a rhythm of courage.

May your days be filled with the warmth of sunlight,
Your nights cradled by the soothing embrace of rest.

May your journey to wellness be guided by grace,
And may you find peace in the healing embrace of time.

In the warmth of the sun's tender rays,
May you be renewed.

May the earth beneath your feet be a steady ground,
Where strength is found.

In the laughter of loved ones,
May joy reside.

May you be held,
In the embrace of gentle hours,
Finding peace within.

You, my dear, are enough—simply by being.

In the quiet chamber of your being,
May healing light be softly gleaming.

Let every cell, resonate within,
Like the sweet strings of a violin.

May strength arise, a sturdy tree,
Rooted deep, for all to see.

On the canvas of your body, colors blend,
A masterpiece of healing, on life's path to mend.

May you be held in a cocoon of soft, iridescent light.
This light—a tender caress of healing and rejuvenation.

May you feel its warmth seeping into your very core,
Dissolving discord and weaving luminosity into your being.

May a happy song echo in your heart,
With the abundance of your wellness.

In the gentle cadence of each breath,
May you hear a serenade of healing.

May you walk a path toward good health with grace,
May it lead you to future vibrant days.

With each dawn, with every breath,
Embrace the gift of another day.

The journey toward robust health begins anew,
And the realm of possibilities lies open.

May your heart be filled with happiness.

May your spirit be uplifted with hope.

May you find strength in challenging times.

May your days be filled with laughter, warmth,
and the company of cherished loved ones.

May you be guided by inner wisdom,
and embrace the beauty of each moment.

May your path be illuminated with love,
and may you feel supported and protected.

As you stand on the threshold of a new beginning,
May the winds of change be gentle, softly spinning.

With each step you take on this uncharted road,
May your heart be light, and your spirit bold.

May your petals dance, may you bloom with grace,
May you drink in beauty in every space.

May your essence inspire hope and delight,
May you grace the world with your gentle light.

May you be protected from harm and strife,
May you grow and thrive in the garden of life.

Blessings to you, dear, in every hour,
May beauty and kindness your heart empower.

May your heart hum with the song of recovery,
As the future stretches before you.

May you embrace this fresh start,
As health returns to you, like an old friend.

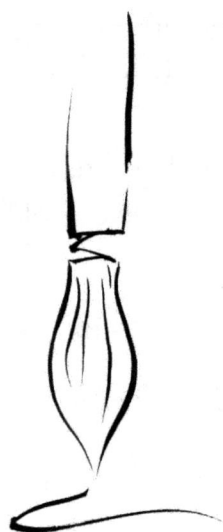

The artist's creation,
Healing through imagination,
Soul's sweet liberation.

May you discover love in every corner of your body,

May you honor the limbs that have carried you this far,

May you grant forgiveness to your ailments and scars,

May you embrace the flesh that cradles your soul's home.

In this chapter unwritten, where your story takes flight,
May your new beginning be a beautiful sight.

Acknowledgments

To The Carers:

The sisters, brothers, parents, children, family, friends,
neighbors, nurses, doctors, health care supporters, thank you!

UP

UPLIFTERS PRESS